WHAT YOU NEED TO KNOW ABOUT
PINK EYE

BY NANCY DICKMANN

CONSULTANT:
MARJORIE J. HOGAN, MD
UNIVERSITY OF MINNESOTA
AND HENNEPIN COUNTY MEDICAL CENTER
ASSOCIATE PROFESSOR OF PEDIATRICS
AND PEDIATRICIAN

CAPSTONE PRESS
a capstone imprint

Fact Finders Books are published by Capstone Press,
1710 Roe Crest Drive, North Mankato, Minnesota 56003
www.mycapstone.com

Library of Congress Cataloging-in-Publication Data
Names: Dickmann, Nancy, author.
Title: What you need to know about pink eye / by Nancy Dickmann.
Other titles: Fact finders. Focus on health.
Description: North Mankato, Minnesota : Capstone Press, a Capstone imprint,
  [2017] | Series: Fact finders. Focus on health | Audience: Ages 8-11. |
  Audience: Grades 4 to 6. | Includes bibliographical references and index.
Identifiers: LCCN 2015045749 |
ISBN 9781491482414 (library binding)
ISBN 9781491482452 (paperback) |
ISBN 9781491482490 (eBook PDF)
Subjects: LCSH: Conjunctivitis--Juvenile literature.
Classification: LCC RE320 .D53 2017 | DDC 617.7/73--dc23
LC record available at http://lccn.loc.gov/2015049743

Produced by Brown Bear Books Ltd.
Editor: Tracey Kelly
Design Manager: Keith Davis
Editorial Director: Lindsey Lowe
Children's Publisher: Anne O'Daly
Picture Manager: Sophie Mortimer
Production Manager: Alastair Gourlay

Photo Credits
Front Cover: Shutterstock: (bottom), Tatiana Makotra (top).
Inside: 1, © Shutterstock/Audrey Arkusha. 3, © Shutterstock/Tatiana Makotra. 4, © Science Photo Library/Dr P. Marazzi.
5, © Shutterstock/Monkey Business Images. 6, © Getty Images/Bigshots. 7 (top), © Thinkstock. 8, © Thinkstock/istockphoto.
10, © Getty Images/Teresa Short. 11, © Dreamstime/Monkey Business Images. 12l, © Science Photo Library/Steve Gschmeissner.
12 (right), © Science Photo Library/Public Health England. 13, © Shutterstock/Image Point France. 14 (top), © Shutterstock/Sergey Novikov. 14 (bottom), © Shutterstock/Sebastian Kaulitzki. 15, © Thinkstock/istockphoto. 16, © Shutterstock/Dragon Images.
17, © Getty Images/William Radcliffe. 18, © Shutterstock/Gos Photodesign. 19, © Dreamstime/Photographer London.
20, ©Shutterstock. 21, © Shutterstock. 22, © Shutterstock/Michael Hanson. 23, © Shutterstock. 24, © Shutterstock/Monkey Business Images. 25 (top), © Thinkstock/Zoonar. 25 (bottom), © Shutterstock. 26, © Shutterstock/Iakov Filimonov. 27, © Getty Images/Tetra Images. 28 (top), © Shutterstock/Adam Gregor. 28 (bottom), © Thinkstock/moodboard. 29, © Shutterstock.

2112

Brown Bear Books has made every attempt to contact the copyright holder.
If anyone has any information please contact licensing@brownbearbooks.co.uk

007686WKTF16

Printed in China

TABLE OF CONTENTS

CHAPTER 1

WHAT IS PINK EYE?

One morning you wake up, and one of your eyes feels itchy. When you look in the mirror, you notice that your eye looks red and puffy. It also might look gooey or crusty, with a thick liquid oozing from it. What is going on?

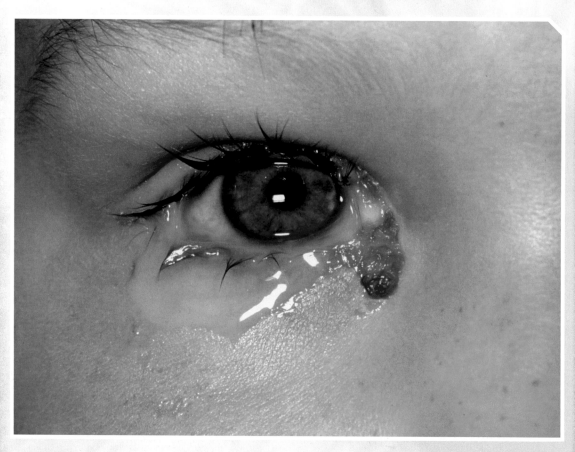

▲ A gooey, sticky eye is one possible sign of pink eye.

▲ Having pink eye won't make you feel ill, so you can still play and be active.

You may have a condition called pink eye. Pink eye is the name that most people give to the illness with a much longer name: Doctors call it conjunctivitis. It is a very common eye problem that affects both children and adults, and even babies too. It can cause redness and itching, as well as swelling and gooey liquid. Some people get pink eye in only one eye, and others have it in both. It can be caused by several different things. Although it can be uncomfortable, it is usually easy to treat. Often, pink eye goes away on its own.

HOW YOUR EYES WORK

Your eyes are both complicated and amazing. Your eyeballs are made up of many parts, each of which has a job to do in helping you see.

An eyeball is about the size and shape of a table tennis ball. What you see when you look in a mirror is just the front part of the eye. The white part is called the **sclera**, and it is the outer coating of the eyeball. The colored part of the eye is called the **iris**. The iris is attached to muscles that make it open and close. The black part in the center is actually a hole called the **pupil**, which lets light into the eyeball.

▲ Irises come in many colors, from blue and green to brown and hazel.

▶ Your eyes can adjust to see things clearly, whether they are near or far away.

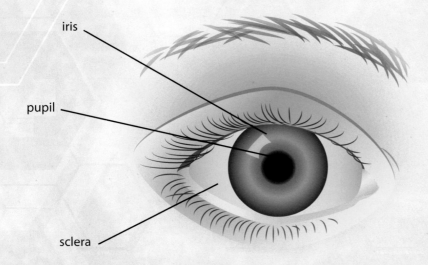

iris

pupil

sclera

◀ When you look at a person's eyes, you can easily see the iris, pupil, and sclera.

conjunctiva—the part of the eye that lines the inside of the eyelid and the front part of the eyeball

inflammation—a condition in which a body part becomes red, swollen, and painful

sclera—the white outer layer of the eyeball

iris—the colored part of the eyeball

pupil—the small, dark opening in the center of the eye

CONJUNCTIVA

The **cornea** sits in front of the iris and pupil. It is clear and helps the eye focus. Just behind the iris and pupil is the lens, which is also see-through. It is curved, like the lens in a telescope. The lens helps to focus light rays as an image on the back of the eyeball. From there, an image is changed into signals the brain can understand.

▲ Like the conjuctiva, the lining of your nose is also a mucous membrane. It produces nasal mucus ("snot").

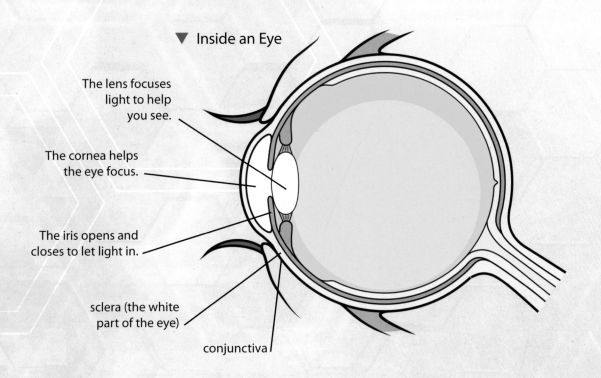

▼ Inside an Eye

The lens focuses light to help you see.

The cornea helps the eye focus.

The iris opens and closes to let light in.

sclera (the white part of the eye)

conjunctiva

But what about the conjunctiva? You see it every time you look in a mirror, without even realizing it! It is made from thin, mostly see-through layers that cover the front of your eyeball. The layers also fold back to line the inside of your eyelids. A conjunctiva is a **mucous membrane**, which is a type of body tissue that produces goo called mucus. This membrane produces a sticky substance that helps keep your eye moist and lubricated.

cornea—the clear outer covering of the eyeball

mucous membrane—a thin layer of cells that produces a type of goo called mucus

DEALING WITH PINK EYE

When the conjunctiva becomes inflamed for any reason, it can lead to conjunctivitis. This inflammation can make the **blood vessels** more visible. Since the blood inside blood vessels is red, the white part of your eye looks red or pink.

HEALTH FACT

Children with pink eye often stay home from school. In the United States, about 3 million school days are missed each year because of pink eye.

▲ There are several different reasons that eyes can look red. Conjunctivitis is only one of them.

▲ Some schools have a rule that says children with pink eye must stay at home, to avoid passing it on to other children.

Pink eye is easy to pass on from one person to another, so it is very common. However, the **symptoms** are usually mild. It can sometimes cause more serious problems but only in very rare cases. Many cases of pink eye will go away on their own. But sometimes you will need to see a doctor for treatment. Pink eye has several different causes. The treatment will depend on what is causing your pink eye.

blood vessel—a tiny tube inside the body that blood travels through. The body's blood vessels stretch thousands of miles.

symptom—something different you notice about your body, suggesting that there is an illness or health problem

CHAPTER 2

WHAT CAUSES PINK EYE?

Pink eye can be caused by various things. **Viruses** cause many cases of pink eye. A virus is a tiny living thing that can cause illnesses. Viruses cannot grow or make copies of themselves on their own. Instead, they need to invade the **cells** of another living thing. Many colds and sore throats are caused by viruses. The same types of viruses can cause pink eye. Other cases of pink eye are caused by **bacteria**.

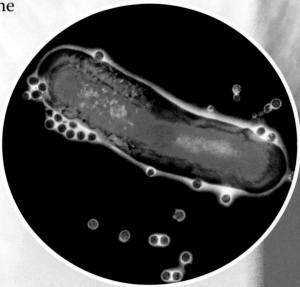

▲ A type of virus called an adenovirus may cause pink eye.

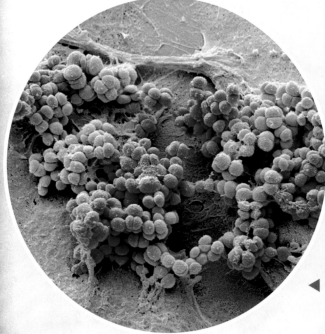

◄ Staphylococcus aureus is a bacteria that can cause pink eye, as well as food poisoning and skin infections.

◀ Your doctor can look inside your ear to tell if you have an ear infection.

Like viruses, bacteria are tiny living things that can sometimes cause illness. However, bacteria are bigger and don't need the cells of other living things to make copies of themselves. Conjunctivitis caused by bacteria is more common in children than in adults. It usually makes your eyes gooier than viral conjunctivitis does.

HEALTH FACT

Sometimes a child might have an ear infection and pink eye at the same time. This happens because both of these conditions can be caused by the same type of bacteria.

virus—a tiny living thing that causes disease and can only make copies of itself inside another living thing

cell—the tiniest building block of life. Your body is made up of trillions of cells.

bacterium—a tiny living thing that can sometimes cause illness

OTHER CAUSES

Some cases of pink eye are a type of **allergic reaction**. When someone has allergies, coming into contact with a harmless substance can make their body behave strangely. Your body can respond the same as if the substance is a dangerous **germ**. Sometimes contact with substances such as **pollen**, dust mites, or flakes of animal skin can lead to pink eye. The eyes will look red and feel itchy, and they will produce a lot of tears.

▲ Pollen is a dustlike substance produced by some plants. It can cause pink eye in people with allergies.

◄ Tiny dust mites make up part of household dust. Some people are allergic to dust mite droppings, which can lead to pink eye.

KATIE'S STORY

Katie woke up one morning with one eye that stung and looked red. Soon, the other eye was hurting as well. Katie went to see her doctor, who told her that this was caused by her pollen allergy. The same allergy was making her skin feel itchy too. An allergy medication soothed her symptoms.

▶ People add chlorine to swimming pools to kill bacteria, but the chlorine can sometimes irritate your eyes.

You don't need to have allergies to develop pink eye. It is possible to get it as a reaction to a substance that irritates the eye. Shampoo, smoke, and chlorine from swimming pools can give people red, watery eyes. Sand or an object scratching the eye can also cause pink eye. In this case, it is best to see a health care provider.

allergic reaction—when your body reacts to a harmless substance as though it was a dangerous germ

germ—a tiny living thing, such as a bacterium or virus, that causes disease

pollen—the fine powder made by a plant's flowers. Pollen can trigger allergic reactions in some people.

CATCHING PINK EYE

Some types of pink eye are **contagious**, which means that you can catch them from someone else. For example, the bacteria that cause pink eye are present in the gooey liquid that comes out of your eye. If someone touches this goo and then touches their own eye, they might catch pink eye.

▲ When you touch the same surfaces as someone with pink eye, you may pick up the virus that causes it.

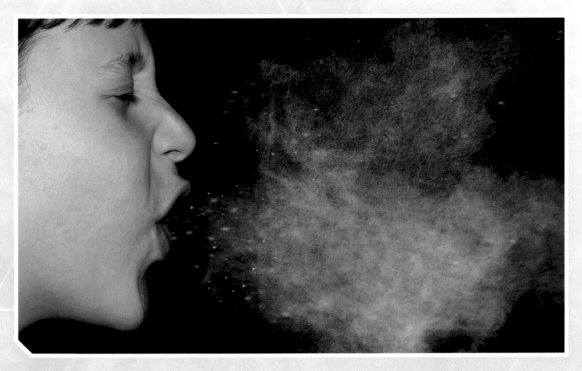

▲ A sneeze can travel a long way very fast
and can send 100,000 germs into the air!

Some of the viruses that cause pink eye are very easy to pass on from one person to another. When a person with this virus sneezes or coughs, they spray out tiny copies of the virus. If you touch a surface where the virus has landed and then your eye, you might get pink eye. Not all types of pink eye are contagious, though. If someone has pink eye caused by an allergy or chlorine, you cannot catch it from them.

contagious—able to be passed on from one person to another

CHAPTER 3

DO YOU HAVE PINK EYE?

No matter what causes it, the symptoms of pink eye are similar. The main symptom is a red or pink eye that may be painful and itchy. The eye may water more than normal, especially if the pink eye was caused by an allergy. The eye may also be sensitive to light. Pink eye caused by bacteria may have a green or yellow gooey discharge. The eye may be crusted shut with dried goo in the morning.

▶ Even if your eyes are itchy, you should try your best not to rub them.

Pink eye often appears in only one eye at first, although it can quickly spread to the other eye. If your pink eye is caused by a virus, that same virus may also give you a cold. Then, you may also have symptoms such as coughing, sneezing, or a runny nose.

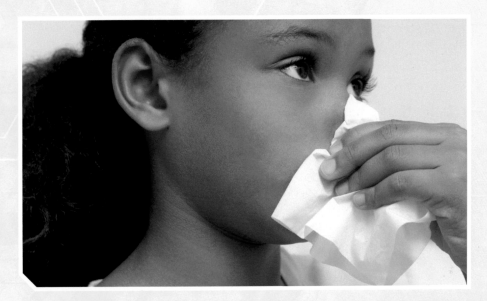

▲ Conjunctivitis often goes along with a cold.

JOHNNY'S STORY

Johnny had red, watery eyes with swollen eyelids. In the mornings, his eyes were crusted shut. The redness faded during the day but would be back again the next morning. His doctor said that it was pink eye caused by a virus and that it would clear up by itself. After a week, he was better.

SEEING A DOCTOR

If you think you have pink eye, it's a good idea to see a doctor. He or she will be able to confirm whether it is pink eye and may be able to tell you what caused it. You should definitely see a doctor if your eyes are painful and sensitive to light, or if your vision is blurred. These can be symptoms of other conditions that may require treatment.

▲ It will not hurt when the doctor looks at your eyes.

Symptom Checklist

- Red, itchy eyes
- A gritty feeling in the eye
- Gooey discharge that may form a crust overnight
- Watery eyes
- Sensitivity to light

The doctor will ask questions about your general health and your current symptoms. He or she will look at your eyes and try to figure out what is causing the pink eye. In a few cases, the doctor may take a sample of any goo to test. He or she will tell you what to do to treat your pink eye and may prescribe medicine.

▶ Scientists can usually figure out what type of bacteria or virus is causing a case of pink eye.

CHAPTER 4
TREATING PINK EYE

Many cases of pink eye go away without the need for treatment. If your pink eye was caused by an allergy, it will clear up once you've removed the allergic substance. If your pink eye was caused by a pollen allergy, then staying away from the source should help. Your doctor may suggest using eye drops or allergy medication to help reduce the symptoms.

▲ If an animal allergy caused your pink eye, try to avoid animals until it goes away completely.

If your pink eye was caused by exposure to chlorine or another irritating substance, then the situation is the same. Removing the irritant, such as by staying out of the swimming pool, will usually help the pink eye to clear up quickly.

◀ Even if pink eye wasn't caused by contacts, leaving them out until it goes away can help your eyes feel better.

OTHER TREATMENTS

If your pink eye was caused by a virus, it will often clear up within a week or two. This will probably happen even without medicine. Your body's **immune system** is good at fighting off viruses such as those that cause colds, flu, and pink eye. Your doctor may give you eye drops to relieve dryness. In a few serious cases, you may be prescribed a medicine that attacks viruses.

▶ If your pink eye is caused by a virus, the pharmacist will probably not recommend an oral medicine.

TANYA'S STORY

Tanya had pink eye, and her doctor recommended letting it clear up by itself. To help with the symptoms, her dad used cotton balls and cooled boiled water to wipe her eyes. The pink eye went away within a week.

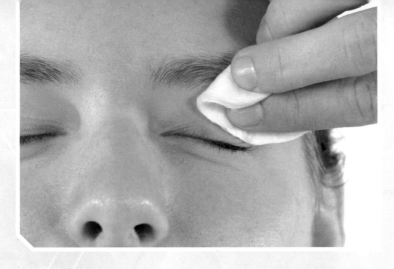

◀ Use a damp cotton pad or ball to wipe away any crustiness from your eye.

If bacteria caused your pink eye, it can be treated by medicines called **antibiotics**, which kill bacteria. They can be given as eye drops or as an **ointment** to be rubbed around the eye. Your doctor may suggest waiting to see if the pink eye clears up on its own before using antibiotics.

▶ Antibiotic drops can help you recover more quickly, giving you less chance to pass pink eye on to other people.

immune system—the system that protects the body by finding and destroying germs

antibiotic—a medicine that is able to kill bacteria

ointment—a soft, oily substance made to rub into the skin. Some ointments contain medicines such as antibiotics.

DON'T PASS IT ON!

Cases of pink eye that are caused by viruses or bacteria are very contagious. That means that it's easy to pass from one person to another. If you have this type of pink eye, you should do your best to avoid passing it on to anyone else. Your school may have a rule that you need stay at home unless you have a note from your doctor.

▶ Things such as door handles, which get touched by many people's hands, often have germs on them.

▲ A hand sanitizer gel contains alcohol, which kills many types of bacteria and viruses.

There are things you can do to stop the spread of pink eye. First, wash your hands often with soap and warm water. If there is no sink available, use a hand sanitizer gel. You should also avoid touching or rubbing your eyes. The germs that cause pink eye can get on your hands. Germs can then be passed to someone else when they touch something that you have already touched. Washing your hands often will make this less likely to happen. Make sure not to share towels, washcloths, blankets, or pillowcases.

PREVENTING PINK EYE

If a friend or family member has pink eye, there are steps you can take to avoid catching it. Don't touch his or her face or eyes, and wash your hands well after you play together. Don't share anything that might go near the eyes, such as towels, sunglasses, hats, or pillows. If someone has pink eye, their bedding and towels should be washed in hot water to kill the germs. Regular hand washing will help keep you and your family germ-free.

▲ Don't reuse a tissue; throw it away once you've used it. Then wash your hands!

▶ If you have pink eye, the germs that cause it can get transferred to your pillowcase. Washing the pillowcase in hot water should kill the germs.

PINK EYE TOP TIPS

DO

DO use a tissue when you cough or sneeze. Then throw it away, and wash your hands with soap.

DO scrub your hands with soap for at least 20 seconds when you wash them.

DON'T

DON'T rub or touch your eyes, even if they itch.

DON'T share glasses or anything that goes on your face, such as sunscreen, moisturizer, or makeup.

► To make sure you've scrubbed for long enough, sing "Happy Birthday" twice to yourself while you do it!

GLOSSARY

allergic reaction (uh-LER-jik ree-AK-shun)—when your body reacts to a harmless substance as though it was a dangerous germ

antibiotic (an-tie-bye-OT-ik)—a medicine that can kill bacteria

bacterium (bak-TEE-ree-uhm)—a tiny living thing that can sometimes cause illness

blood vessel (BLOOD VESS-ul)—a tiny tube inside the body that blood travels through

cell (SELL)—the tiniest building block of life

conjunctiva (con-junk-TIE-vuh)—the part of the eye that lines the inside of the eyelid and the front part of the eyeball

contagious (kun-TAY-jus)—able to be passed on from one person to another

cornea (KOR-nee-uh)—the clear outer covering of the eyeball

germ (JURM)—a tiny living thing, such as a bacterium or virus

immune system (i-MYOON SIS-tum)—the system that protects the body by finding and destroying germs

inflammation (in-fluh-MAY-shun)—a condition in which a body part becomes red, swollen, and painful

iris (EYE-riss)—the colored part of the eyeball

mucous membrane (MYOO-kuss MEM-brain)—a thin layer of cells that produces a type of goo called mucus

ointment (OYNT-ment)—a soft, oily subtance made to rub into the skin. Some ointments contain medicines such as antibiotics.

pollen (PAH-len)—the fine powder made by a plant's flowers. Pollen can trigger allergic reactions in some people.

pupil (PYOO-pill)—the small, dark opening in the center of the eye

sclera (SKLER-uh)—the white outer layer of the eyeball

symptom (SIMP-tum)—something that happens in the body, suggesting that there is an illness or health problem

virus (VIE-russ)—a tiny living thing that causes disease

READ MORE

Amsel, Sheri. *The Everything Kids' Human Body Book.* Avon, Mass.: Adams Media, 2012.

DK Publishing. *Human Body: A Visual Encyclopedia.* New York: Dorling Kindersley, 2012.

Rhatigan, Joe. *Ouch!: The Weird & Wild Ways Your Body Deals with Agonizing Aches, Ferocious Fevers, Lousy Lumps, Crummy Colds, Bothersome Bites, Breaks, Bruises & Burns.* Watertown, Mass.: Imagine Publishing, 2013.

Spilsbury, Louise. *Sight.* The Science Behind. North Mankato, Minn.: Capstone, 2012.

INTERNET SITES

FactHound offers a safe, fun way to find Internet sites related to this book. All of the sites on FactHound have been researched by our staff.

Here's all you do:

Visit *www.facthound.com*

Type in this code: 978149182414

 Check out projects, games and lots more at **www.capstonekids.com**

INDEX